100% GLEEK: THE UNOFFICIAL GUIDE TO GLEE
A BANTAM BOOK 978 0 553 82274 8
First published in Great Britain by Bantam,
an imprint of Random House Children's Books
A Random House Group Company
Bantam edition published 2010
3 5 7 9 10 8 6 4 2
Text copyright © Bantam, 2010

Design by Shubrook Bros. Creative www.shubrookbros.com
Bantam Books are published by Random House Children's Books,
61–63 Uxbridge Road, London W5 5SA
www.rbooks.co.uk, www.kidsatrandomhouse.co.uk
Addresses for companies within The Random House Group Limited can be found at: www.randomhouse.co.uk/offices.htm
THE RANDOM HOUSE GROUP Limited Reg. No. 954009
A CIP catalogue record for this book is available from the British Library

Printed in the UK

THE UNOFFICIAL GUIDE TO GLEE!

100% gleek

BANTAM BOOKS

Evie Parker

CONTENTS

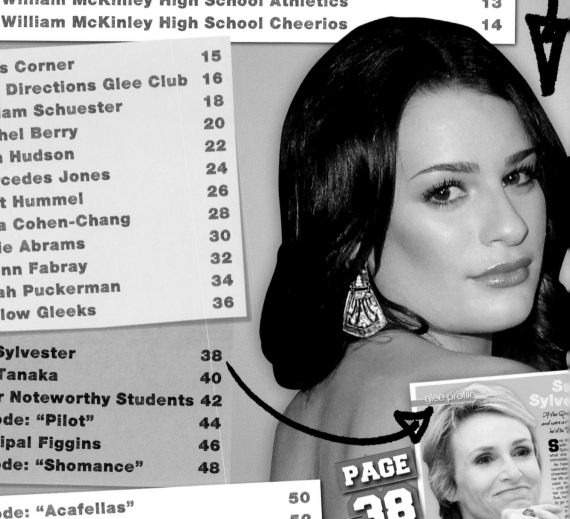

Rachel Berry, the queen of glee club.

glee profile

Sue Sylvester

PAGE 38

Sue Sylvester... the Grinch in disguise?

She makes it her mission to bring down New Directions and ruin Will Schuester's life in the process.

Mercedes – she ain't no Kelly Rowland!

Check out the school administration and faculty!

faculty

WILLIAM McKINLEY HIGH SCHOOL

THUNDERCLAP

2010 Yearbook

William McKinley High School
Lima, Ohio

School **Administration** and **Faculty**

Principal Figgins
Principal

Emma Pillsbury
Guidance counselor

William Schuester
Spanish teacher & director of New Directions glee club

Ken Tanaka
Head Football coach

Sue Sylvester
Head coach of the McKinley award-winning Cheerios

Henri St. Pierre
Woodshop teacher

Find out more about the school student body!

students

WILLIAM McKINLEY HIGH SCHOOL
STUDENT BODY

Rachel Berry
Sophomore
She'd rather be poor than anonymous.

Finn Hudson
He's a natural born leader.

Mercedes Jones
Sophomore
It's Beyoncé all the way for Mercedes.

Artie Abrams
He's wheel-y, wheel-y good.

Quinn Fabray
She's a cheery cheerleader through and through!

Tina Cohen-Chang
Her stutter never stopped her.

Kurt Hummel
Sophomore
He's ALL about the style.

Mike Chang
What a dancer.

Brittany
She's the queen of hairography.

Noah "Puck" Puckerman
He's a pretty rock 'n' roll kind of guy

Santana Lopez
She's one hot chick.

Jacob Ben Israel
His crush on Rachel is immense!

Suzy Pepper
This sassy student has a hankering for Mr Schue.

McKinley Clubs
and
Extra-curricular
Activities

WILLIAM MCKINLEY NEWSPAPER

Gossip blogger: *Jacob Ben Israel*

He's the hack with a nose for a scoop and eyes for Rachel!

CELIBACY CLUB

President: *Quinn Fabray*

Members: *Brittany, Finn Hudson, Jacob Ben Israel, Santana Lopez, Noah "Puck" Puckerman*

SPEECH CLUB

Rachel Berry

MUSLIM STUDENTS CLUB

Rachel Berry

RENAISSANCE CLUB

Rachel Berry

MOCK UNITED NATIONS CLUB

Rachel Berry

Rachel Berry has her hands full!

BLACK STUDENTS UNION

Rachel Berry

12

WILLIAM McKINLEY
HIGH SCHOOL
FOOTBALL TEAM

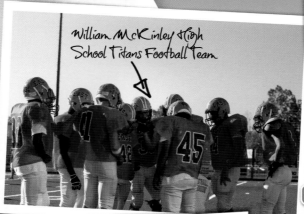

William McKinley High
School Titans Football Team

Head coach: Ken Tanaka

Captain of the team: Finn Hudson

Kicker: Kurt Hummel

Players: Azinio, Mike
Chang, Matt Rutherford,
Noah "Puck" Puckerman

WILLIAM McKINLEY
HIGH SCHOOL
HOCKEY TEAM

William McKinley
High School
Hockey Team

They're chipper and cheery and cheering's their bag, baby!

cheerios

Find out how the Cheerios' coach sees it!

14

WILLIAM McKINLEY HIGH SCHOOL CHEERIOS

Sue's Corner

Coach Sylvester is a guest television commentator with her own segment for the WOHN News 8 local news called *Sue's Corner*.

Sue always manages to bring an interesting perspective to the topic of the day:

"Preggers": Sue talks about how caning – Singapore's preferred method of corporal punishment for minor criminal infractions – should be used in the United States to keep the streets clean and safe. Sue's final word on caning . . . "Yes."

"Throwdown": Sue posits that people marvel at how she is so in touch with the struggle of minorities because she herself is one. Apparently, she is 1/16 Comanche Indian!

"Mash-Up": With the heated battle over gay marriage flaring up all over the country, Sue takes the debate down a path few have explored – people marrying their dogs. Why not, she asks. Sue's final word: Woof, on Prop. 15. Ohio.

"Mattress": Offended by the sizes of regular people out shopping at the malls over the holiday season, Sue asks the state to put a ban on fat people out and about the day after Thanksgiving. She says it would give her poor eyeballs a rest from all those hideous bodies. Happy Holidays to you too, Sue!

And that's how Sue Cs it!

Head coach: Sue Sylvester

Head cheerleader: Quinn Fabray

Squad: Brittany, Santana Lopez, Becky Jackson

Go! Go! Cheerios!
Go! Go! Titans!

NEW DIRECTIONS
glee club

DEFINITION:
Glee -opening
yourself up
to joy!

Director: William Schuester

The gleeks shine
once they get
on stage.

Accompanist: Brad

Singers: Artie Abrams, Rachel Berry, Brittany, Mike Chang, Tina Cohen-Chang, Quinn Fabray, Finn Hudson, Kurt Hummel, Mercedes Jones, Santana Lopez, Noah "Puck" Puckerman, Matt Rutherford

NEW DIRECTIONS
glee club
Road to Sectionals
Performances & Awards

WILLIAM McKINLEY HIGH SCHOOL

ASSEMBLY

 "Push It"

INVITATIONALS

 "Last Name"
lead sung by *April Rhodes*

"Somebody to Love"

SECTIONALS

 "Don't Rain on My Parade"
lead sung by *Rachel Berry*

 "You Can't Always Get What You Want"
lead sung by *Finn Hudson*

 "My Life Would Suck Without You"

New Directions
Winner of the Ohio state show choir sectionals

William "Mr. Schue" Schuester

Mr. Schue is the talented teacher with rhythm in his feet and music in his soul.

Singing is what Will is all about. As a student at William McKinley High School, he helped the glee club win the 1993 National Show Choir Championship cup – it was one of the best moments of his life. But after graduation, he stopped performing, married his high school sweetheart and left college with a safe degree in accounting. A few years later, Will found himself back at McKinley, this time as the school's Spanish teacher. And when choir director Sandy Ryerson is fired for inappropriately touching a student, Will offers his services as a replacement, hopeful that it will capture some of the joy from his youth. Of course, Will gets the job and New Directions is born!

At home, Will tries to balance the needs of his demanding wife Terri (who says she is pregnant with his baby), the anxiety of fatherhood, and the close bond he's forming with fellow McKinley faculty member, Emma Pillsbury.

He helped the glee club win the 1993 National Show Choir Championship cup.

Matthew James Morrison

When life mirrors fiction . . .

Apparently, Morrison's nickname is Matty Fresh!

As a self-professed theatre geek from sunny Fort Ord in California, the young Matthew Morrison spent his school years much like the glee performers from the show, starring in school musicals and plays. The budding star was also voted class president and prom king.

Morrison then attended New York University's Tisch School of the Arts but grew disenchanted and dropped out, only to land himself a role in the Broadway version of *Footloose*. Briefly a member of boy band LMNT, he quit for a role in the stage revival of *The Rocky Horror Picture Show*. In 2002, Morrison finally got his first major role as Link Larkin in the Broadway adaptation of *Hairspray*.

Television roles quickly followed with appearances in *Marci X, Hack,* and *CSI: Miami*. In 2005, Morrison featured in the TV version of *Once Upon a Mattress* alongside Carol Burnett. Following that success he secured a well-earned Tony nomination for his performance as Fabrizio Nacarelli in Adam Guettel's *The Light in the Piazza.*

Film credits also include *Music and Lyrics* as the teen sensation's manager and a policeman in *Dan in Real Life*. In that same year, the actor went back to the stage for the off-Broadway production of *10 Million Miles*. Morrison was soon discovered by the *Glee* series creator Ryan Murphy. Murphy had spent three long months scouting for performers to join his cast and Morrison filled the multi-talented bill for teacher, Will Schuester.

Rachel Berry

She puts the A+ in the conventional Type A personality.

The daughter of gay, Jewish partners Hiram and Leroy Berry, Rachel was born via a surrogate they pre-screened based on their high standards of beauty and IQ. As a little girl, Rachel was told by her fathers that she was meant to lead a special life. She was trained in dance, singing and anything that could give her an edge.

By the time she hit her teens, Rachel's, confidence and laser-like focus made her a social pariah. At McKinley High, her fellow students took great joy in throwing slushies in her face or mocking the videos on her MySpace page.

In Mr. Schue's glee club, Rachel finally found an activity worthy of her talents. Sadly, it didn't improve her social status but she did get to hang out with Finn Hudson, the cute, popular all-star quarterback, whose, sweet vocal stylings impressed Rachel. He soon became the object of her affections. The only problem was his girlfriend, Rachel's number one enemy – Cheerios cheerleader Quinn Fabray.

Finn makes Rachel swoon.

Lea Michele

A talented and vivacious singer who found her way to fame just by chance . . .

Michele was eight when she landed her first Broadway role in Les Misérables.

Born Lea Michele Sarfati in the Bronx, New York, Michele had no early ambition to be a singer. Her lucky break came when she tagged along with a friend to an open audition for a Broadway musical and as they say, fate stepped in.

Michele was just eight when she landed her first Broadway role as the young Cosette in the New York production of *Les Misérables*. Three years later, Michele had a part in the original Broadway cast of *Ragtime*, and parts in *Fiddler on the Roof* and *The Diary of Anne Frank* swiftly followed. However, it was her role as Wendla in the new musical *Spring Awakening* that changed her life. Nominated for a Drama Desk Award for Outstanding Actress in a Musical, Michele won rave reviews from both critics and audiences alike.

While on the west coast, she went along to audition for some television pilots. The second one she read for was *Glee*, and she was instantly cast as high-school vocal diva Rachel Berry. Making the transition from theatre to television, Michele has continued to wow fans with her powerhouse lead vocals. In just one year, this young actress has been nominated for a Golden Globe and a Teen Choice Award. She went on to win a Satellite Award in the Best Actress category and also shared a Screen Actor's Guild award for an Outstanding Performance by an Ensemble in a Comedy Series.

Finn Hudson

He's the jock with a big heart and the voice of an angel.

It would be very easy to assume that Finn, the cute captain of the McKinley Titans football team, would fit the bill as a stereotypical high-school jock/jerk. And while he's been guilty of some nerd torture in his day, Finn also has a big heart that makes him stand up for the little guy. A lot of that empathy comes from his mum. She raised him as a single parent and sacrificed a lot for him, even getting her heart broken, but she still managed to be the best mother she could.

That sense of honour and duty is what helps him deal with the news that his girlfriend, Quinn Fabray, is pregnant, apparently with his baby. Despite being terrified, Finn doesn't run away. Instead, he stands by her, even when he has no idea what the future holds. And even when he discovers Quinn's betrayal and lies about the paternity of her baby, Finn forgives her and stands together with his New Directions family to win in the end.

The super-cute, clean-cut captain of McKinley's football team.

Cory Monteith

The rebel who found his thespian niche.

There's a world of difference between the on-screen all-American persona of Finn Hudson and the real-life, hot actor Cory Monteith. First of all, Monteith is a Canadian boy from Calgary. Secondly, while Finn leads a pretty conventional life, Montieth has something of a rebel's soul.

Montieth says his first job was at a car lot at the tender age of 13. He disliked school so much he decided to drop out and worked odd jobs at Wal-Mart, in construction and even as a cabbie! But it wasn't long before he stumbled into acting where his striking good looks served him well. It was the filmmaker David DeCoteau who discovered the actor and cast him in horror film *Killer Bash*. Monteith moved to Vancouver, where he gained guest roles on *Stargate: Atlantis*, *Supernatural* and *Smallville*. He also featured in *Final Destination 3*, *White Noise 2* and *Bloody Mary*, until 2006 when he secured a recurring role on the ABC drama *Kyle XY*.

When the role of Finn Hudson came around for *Glee*, Monteith says his only musical ability was his prowess on the drums so he used them to audition. He says he'd never even sung before that day, but the casting agents and producers heard plenty of potential in Montieth's passionate vocals. They snatched him up and in the past year Monteith admits his castmates have been schooling him on the necessary Broadway 101 knowledge he needs.

Cory once worked as a cabbie!

23

Mercedes Jones

This feisty, sassy singer has a set of pipes that could blow the roof off an auditorium!

Mercedes Jones is one girl who knows she was not brought into this world to play second fiddle to anyone. While she may not have the slender body of vocal rival Rachel Berry, Mercedes has the talent to make heads turn. When she joins glee it's to take centre stage, but she's had to learn the valuable lessons of patience and humility. Mr. Schuester is one teacher who honours everyone's talent.

Mercedes has had to struggle with peer persecution for her weight, which is one reason why she and Kurt Hummel get on so well. Together they can make beautiful music and have each other's back when the outside world chooses not to accept them.

Kurt and Mercedes are the BFFs that found each other through glee.

Amber Riley

A relative unknown, Amber has shot to stardom in a blaze of glee!

Starring in *Glee* has put Amber Riley on the professional map. Originally From Los Angeles, Riley says her mother realized her vocal gifts at the age of two and invested in lessons to help shape her abilities. But it wasn't always easy for the full-figured Riley to pursue her singing, especially in a city where how you look almost always determines your initial success. Riley openly admits the audition process was hard on her self-esteem growing up, so she decided to step away from it until she felt ready to handle all the pressure of the business.

In her teens, a more confident Riley jumped back into the fray and at the age of 17 went for an *American Idol* audition. Shockingly, Riley didn't make it through the first round, so she never saw Simon Cowell and his crew. The songstress admits it was a hard blow, but she credits the rejection as galvanizing her resolve to become a better vocalist.

Amber auditioned for American Idol.

She won a small part in the TV project *St. Sass*, but it wasn't until *Glee* that things changed. Last to the casting process for the show, Riley says that she wasn't aware she was auditioning for a co-lead role until she arrived. She put her all into bringing Mercedes Jones to life and the producers absolutely loved it. She was cast, and like a good diva-in-training, the hugely talented singer, and admittedly ever improving dancer, has just never looked back.

Kurt Hummel

From his fabulous car to his perfect outfits, Kurt never does anything half-heartedly.

While all the regular students of McKinley High trudge about in their jeans, T-shirts and team uniforms, Kurt Hummel prides himself on setting the bar high when it comes to clothes and style.

The popular crowd likes to torture Kurt for his "girly" ways, but he knows who he is and waves his gay banner proudly. And while he lost his mum at a young age, Kurt's manly father, Burt, supports his son 100% – even if he doesn't always understand him. But once he joins glee, Kurt finds like-minded friends, from BFF Mercedes Jones to the oddly empathetic Finn Hudson. In glee club he can be bolder, more confident, and can truly live the words of his favourite song, "Defying Gravity".

In glee club Kurt finds like-minded

Chris Colfer

An actor with easy charm and self-assured nature that belies his high-school years.

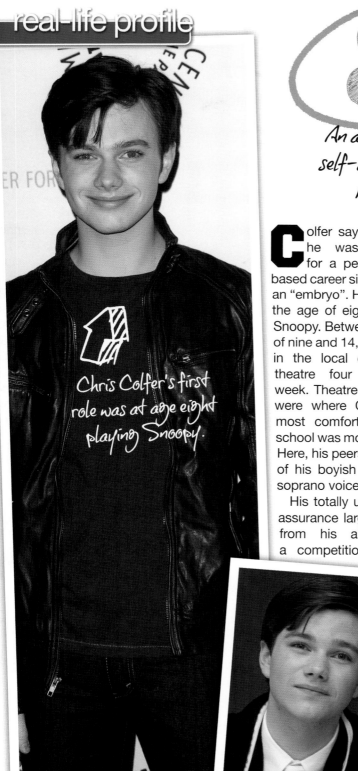

Chris Colfer's first role was at age eight playing Snoopy.

Colfer says he knew he was destined for a performance-based career since he was an "embryo". He began at the age of eight, playing Snoopy. Between the age of nine and 14, he worked in the local community theatre four nights a week. Theatre and home were where Colfer was most comfortable; high school was more difficult. Here, his peers made fun of his boyish looks and soprano voice.

His totally unflappable assurance largely stems from his abilities as a competition debater for which he won three championship titles. At high school he was also part of the drama club and president of the writing club in which he wrote original plays like *Shirley Todd,* a spoof of Sondheim's *Sweeney Todd*. By the age of 15, Colfer and his parents started trucking down to Los Angeles to audition for professional parts.

It wasn't until *Glee* that Colfer's audition fortunes really changed. Originally, Chris read for the part of Artie Abrams, but when he got into the room with the series creator Ryan Murphy, things changed. Murphy immediately saw a likeness between Chris and the iconic role of Kurt Von Trapp from *The Sound of Music*. The pair talked, and Murphy found a kindred spirit in the young actor that reminded him of himself as a young man. He went back and crafted the role of Kurt Hummel for Chris and cast him as the talented student sure of his voice, style and gay sexuality.

27

Tina Cohen-Chang

A reluctant star who's set to shine.

In the halls of McKinley High School, Tina Cohen-Chang might be a wallflower that likes to slip into the shadows, but in glee club her voice prefers to step out and take command of the spotlight. Part of the goth crowd, Tina is more comfortable existing in the fringe, away from the popular crew. She's always had a stutter that comes out during stressful situations, so she's careful about what and when she says anything. But give her a big song and some dance moves, and Tina comes alive. She finds a kindred spirit in Artie Abrams, a fellow oddball who follows the beat of his own drum. In a moment alone, she actually confesses to him that her stutter is an act due to her shyness. He doesn't take it well since it's a lie, which leaves their friendship on shaky ground.

Her friend, Artie – a fellow oddball.

Jenna Ushkowitz

An unconventional path to Hollywood...

Jenna and Lea Michele have been friends since they were eight years old!

Originally from Seoul, South Korea, Jenna was adopted by the Ushkowitz family of East Meadow, Long Island, New York. At the age of three, her parents got her a manager who quickly booked the three-year-old tot in national TV commercials.

In her teens, Jenna attended Holy Trinity Diocesan High School because of its stellar theatre department, where she starred as Little Red Riding Hood in *Into the Woods*, Romaine Patterson in *The Laramie Project* and other productions like *Les Misérables*. But by then, she had already made her Broadway debut in the 1996 revival of *The King and I* starring Lou Diamond Phillips.

In 2006 Ushkowitz finally worked professionally with Lea Michele (the pair have been friends since they were eight) when she was cast to understudy multiple roles in the Broadway hit *Spring Awakening*. As it turns out, the New York casting associate for *Glee* also ran the casting for *Spring Awakening*! Ushkowitz openly admits she thought she had totally flubbed her first audition for the hit show but the producers disagreed and flew her out to Los Angeles. Ryan Murphy loved her edgy vulnerability so they cast her as their Asian goth with a faux stutter.

Artie Abrams

A talented singer with boundless courage and spirit.

To most people the idea of a kid in a wheelchair singing and dancing in a glee club would seem a little unlikely. But for Artie Abrams, his wheelchair is an impediment that just can't block his talent. Abrams lost his ability to walk, and his mum, to a car crash when he was eight.

A tragic event like that would have stunted most people, but not Artie. An eternal optimist, he hasn't let his disability stop him from pursuing his dreams. Even after he gets picked on by the football jocks, Artie just picks himself and his chair back up and gets on with things. It's that hopeful spirit that Will Schuester clearly recognized in Artie when he auditioned for glee club, and it's the backbone for the team's endless courage.

His wheelchair is an impediment that just can't block his talent.

Kevin McHale

A multi-talented singer and dancer.

Although gleek Artie might be confined to his wheelchair, in real life, actor Kevin McHale is blessed to have full mobility. In fact, McHale's first career was as a singing and dancing member of the boy band NLT (Not Like Them). The Plano, Texas, native found his love of performing early doing local commercials but he never thought it would ever turn into an actual career.

In 2003 McHale met up with the fellow members of NLT and they were signed to a label. Inspired by a very distinct R&B/pop sound, "That Girl" was their first single to be released in 2007. They went on a tour of the United States, opening for the chart-topping Pussycat Dolls. Sadly for fans, NLT broke up in 2009, but by then McHale had moved on to new opportunities.

Having relocated to Los Angeles, McHale landed guest spots on hit series like NBC's *The Office*, *Zoey 101* and *True Blood*. McHale says his manager sent him out to audition for the pilot of *Glee* because it was one of the rare projects that included singing and acting. Little did he know that he would get the part, which would have him doing it all sitting in a wheelchair!

McHale relocated to Los Angeles, where his career really took off.

Quinn Fabray

Quintessential mean girl or just misunderstood?

At first sight, Quinn Fabray is just a typical mean girl. Blonde, gorgeous, head cheerleader for the Cheerios and comfortably seated at the top of the social ladder, nothing could go wrong for Quinn Fabray . . . until she finds out that she's pregnant.

Suddenly, her perfect world starts to come apart as she learns the baby is not Finn Hudson's (her boyfriend of five months), but Noah Puckerman's from a one-night stand. The pregnancy also jeopardizes her spot on Sue Sylvester's Cheerios, the loss of which would mean social suicide. So she joins glee club to spy for Sue, but ends up finding a new family amongst the talented misfits.

Who's the daddy?

Dianna Agron

A natural born actress who has always had Hollywood firmly in her sights.

Dianna Agron was born in the state of Georgia but then raised in San Francisco, California. She took the musical theatre path in school, performing in all the plays she could. In high school, she taught dance on the side and saved the money to fund her move to Los Angeles. Agron bravely decided to jump right into the profession that fuelled her passions.

A firm believer in taking chances, she worked tirelessly until she landed a small part in the 2005 film *Talkers Are No Good Doers*. From there she started getting guest roles in hit series like *CSI: NY*, *Shark* and a recurring role in *Veronica Mars*. Her friendship with fellow actor Milo Ventimiglia led to a role in his directorial project *It's a Mall World* and then a recurring role as Debbie Marshall in the first season of the NBC series *Heroes*.

But nothing was a regular gig until she got called in to read for the new high school musical dramedy *Glee*. She admits she was so freaked out before the audition she almost ditched it. Luckily for her, she powered through the nerves and wowed the casting team with her take on angelic bad girl, Quinn Fabray.

Raised in San Francisco, Dianna didn't have far to travel to move to Los Angeles.

Noah "Puck" Puckerman

This boy is one hot playa!

A pretty face with a hot, toned body means open season for this high-school hottie, whether you're a cougar on Puck's pool-cleaning route or the annoying lead singer for New Directions.

Part of the McKinley High cool clique, Puck is a member of the football team. In his free time he likes to torture the school nerds with slushie assaults, trash-bin dumpings or porta-loo flippings. He'd never admit it, but Puck has it bad for Quinn, who he gets pregnant after a one-night stand. But despite his feelings, Puck just can't stop his alley-cat ways. And when Puck joins glee and struts his stuff onstage, well, he just gets even hotter.

Puck has a big crush on Quinn Fabray.

34

Mark Salling

Singing, song writing and acting – Salling's skills are limitless.

Mark worked as a guitar teacher before becoming a songwriter.

Music has always been the dominant creative thread in Mark Salling's life. Born and raised in Dallas, Texas, Salling started playing the piano at the age of five, writing his own original songs at the tender age of six. Influenced by all types of music, Salling worked at his craft as a guitar teacher and session player in Texas before he graduated into songwriting for American artists like Josh Green and Danielle McKee.

Shortly after his high school graduation, Salling attended the Los Angeles Music Academy and tried to get his own music career off the ground. In 2008 he released an album called *Jericho* but it didn't take off as hoped. Salling decided to send out headshots with the aim of getting cast as an extra who could play guitar in television shows and film projects. Fortunately, an agent picked him up and submitted him for the pilot casting of *Glee*. The rest is Puck history.

Salling says in his time off from *Glee* he'll continue to pursue his personal music and hopes to put together an album in the future.

Puck's Mohawk hairstyle was Salling's idea.

FELLOW GLEEKS

Brittany
(Heather Morris)

Not the brightest bulb at McKinley.

Ask her fellow Cheerios and gleek buddies why Brittany only goes by her first name, and they'd probably tell you she forgot her last one. She's not the brightest bulb at McKinley, but the girl certainly has some hot moves. Whether she's flying through the air as a Cheerio or prancing with precision on stage with show choir, Brittany sure is a choreographer's dream. She kills it backing up Kurt with some sharp Beyoncé moves and flies into the splits like a gifted gymnast. Just don't ask the girl the square root of four (rainbows!?) or how to bake . . . anything. While she straddles two worlds as a Cheerio and a gleek, her loyalty to the nerdy kind is still up in the air so they'd better watch out for this one!

Santana Lopez
(Naya Rivera)

Santana's a saucy spitfire that knows how to shake up the opposite sex (and quite possibly her own gender too). She learned bitchy 101 from the best – Quinn Fabray – during their Cheerios days and she's not afraid to lash out. Be it Kurt's sexuality or Puck's lousy credit score, Santana will judge everyone with a withering comment and walk away with a smile. Yet she seems to be exhibiting a fondness for glee club beyond her espionage assignment from Sue Sylvester. She's got a great voice and smooth moves which can only make New Directions stronger. And she gets to hang out with her BFF Brittany, who also seems to be a friend with benefits – whoa there, lady!

Mike Chang
(Harry Shum, Jr.)

Dubiously dubbed "the Other Asian" by Sue Sylvester, Mike Chang is certainly a lot more than just his ethnicity. Known primarily as a good football player, Chang breaks out of his mould when he joins the show choir where he can express all the hidden creative spirit that's inside him. A constant source of comedy laughs, he lightens the mood during heavy rehearsals. He's also got some pop 'n' lock moves that will totally blow you away.

Matt Rutherford
(Dijon Talton)

Mighty Matt Rutherford is another one of the brave football players that joined Finn Hudson in New Directions. Despite some ridicule, he's letting out his inner singer and dancer and can be found strutting his talented stuff with pride in glee club.

Brad
(Brad Ellis)

The McKinley pianist.

There might be song in glee club, but there would be no music without the fantastic accompaniment of Brad, the McKinley High pianist. He's there at every practice to lend some melodic backbone to New Directions' awesome voices. In reality, Brad is actually Brad Ellis, a really talented composer and an important member of *Glee*'s music production team.

Sue Sylvester

If the Grinch weren't green and wore a red tracksuit, then he'd be Sue Sylvester.

Sue is definitely a teacher with the disposition of a tyrant. Sylvester is used to getting what she wants through terror, intimidation and muscle.

As head coach of McKinley's nationally honoured Cheerios cheerleader squad, Sue relishes her life under the spotlight. She's used to winning all the time – until Will Schuester steps into her circle. As driven as Sue, he's the first person in aeons to go toe-to-toe with her so he can get his glee club off the ground. Unwilling to give an inch of her budget or attention away to benefit a rival club, Sue makes it her mission to bring down New Directions and ruin Will Schuester's life in the process.

Sue makes it her mission to bring down New Directions and ruin Will Schuester's life in the process.

Jane Lynch

A veteran comedian, character actress and improv genius.

Jane has played many parts throughout her career.

Jane Lynch has been wowing audiences and critics for more than 20 years.

Jane Lynch has wowed audiences and critics for more than 20 years. Born and raised in Illinois, Lynch grew up knowing that she wanted to be a performer. She got a degree in Theatre and an MFA in Theatre from Cornell.

One of her first roles to catch attention was playing Carol Brady in the popular *Real Live Brady Bunch* stage show.

In the 90s she started getting cast in guest roles on television shows and in the early 2000s, director and writer Christopher Guest cast her as lesbian dog breeder Christy Cummings, for his mockumentary *Best in Show*. She was a hit and the pair went on to collaborate in films like *A Mighty Wind* and *For Your Consideration*.

Those films drew the attention of Judd Apatow who cast her in *The 40 Year Old Virgin*, and

Talladega Nights: The Ballad of Ricky Bobby. Recently, she has featured in films like *Role Models*, *Ice Age: Dawn of the Dinosaurs*, and *Alvin and the Chipmunks*.

She and her fellow *Glee* cast members won the SAG Award in 2010 for Outstanding Performance by an Ensemble in a Comedy Series. Lynch is happily married to her long-term partner Dr. Lara Embry.

Ken Tanaka

He'd do anything for the love of a good woman.

Coach Ken Tanaka might not be the most handsome, worldly or romantic guy, but he's a good man. Sure, being the head coach of a pretty lousy high-school football team means most of his decisions come from a testosterone-infused point of view, but he tries to do what's best for the kids and the school. When he takes the wrong path, like spitting on Emma Pillsbury's car after she initially refuses to date him or changing football practice so it conflicts with glee club, Tanaka's conscience usually gets the better of him and he always does his best to make amends.

He really likes car shows and a cappella singing, leading to his short stint in Acafellas. But most of all he loves the pretty, germ-challenged Emma Pillsbury. Sadly Ken has set himself up for heartbreak, by pursuing her when he knows she is totally devoted to Will Schuester.

Ken hearts Emma – but her heart belongs elsewhere . . .

Patrick Gallagher

He's been around the block.

As an actor from Chilliwack, British Columbia, Canada, Patrick Gallagher's been a familiar face in Canada for more than 15 years. A graduate from the National Theatre School of Canada in Quebec, Gallagher then moved to Toronto where he got his first professional job in the world premiere stage production of *The Nightingale* at the Young People's Theatre.

In the 90s, Gallagher was a frequent guest star on numerous television shows like *RoboCop: The Series*, *Forever Knight*, *F/X: The Series*, *La Femme Nikita* and *Due South* to name just a few.

In 2003, the actor drew favourable attention for his supporting role as Awkward Davies in the hit film *Master and Commander: The Far Side of the World* starring Russell Crowe. And the following year he played Gary the Bartender in the indie smash hit *Sideways*.

Before he landed *Glee*, Gallagher featured as Attila the Hun in the blockbuster *Night at the Museum* films starring Ben Stiller and Robin Williams. Older *Glee* fans will also recognize Gallagher for his work as Erik Northman's vampire guard Chow in the hit show *True Blood*.

With the success of *Glee*, Gallagher now splits his time between Los Angeles and Canada.

Patrick Gallagher's been a familiar face in Canada for more than 15 years.

WILLIAM McKINLEY HIGH SCHOOL

OTHER NOTEWORTHY STUDENTS

Jacob Ben Israel
(Josh Sussman)

When you think nerd at McKinley, just think Jacob. From the Jew-fro to his inappropriate comments, he's the ultimate awkward teen. As the gossip blogger for the school newspaper, Israel can always sniff out a good secret. While he may be necessary for good reviews and positive spin, Jacob certainly isn't wanted by any social clique. Of course, that probably wouldn't be the case if he wasn't so icky and creepy. His obsessive crush on Rachel Berry might be considered cute until he ruins it by asking her to flash her bra for a story or trying to get a pair of her underwear. However, Jacob does have some redeeming qualities. At Sectionals, he bravely stepped in for Finn at the last minute – it's just a shame he peed himself with nerves when he got there. Eww!

He told Rachel to show him her bra! Poor, poor Rachel.

Suzy Pepper
(Sarah Drew)

Suzy Pepper, another obsessive student with "issues", locked her sights on poor Mr. Schue and got seriously delusional about her chances of winning his heart. She'd doodle their names together on her notebook and look for any opportunity to corner him. She once gave him a neck-tie with peppers on it to remind him of her and then phone-stalked him. Of course, Terri Schuester put a stop to the calls. That triggered poor Suzy's downward spiral, and in a failed suicide attempt she popped one of the world's hottest peppers into her mouth and went into a medically-induced coma for three days. It took two years of intense therapy but Pepper eventually returned to McKinley and was even able to shake Schuester-smitten Rachel Berry from her very own inappropriate crush.

Suzy Pepper is H.O.T for Mr. Schue!

She doodles love notes in her notebook.

Suzy Pepper 4 Mr. Schue
X X
x

"PILOT"

Writer(s): Ryan Murphy, Brad Falchuk, Ian Brennan
Director: Ryan Murphy
Guest Stars: Stephen Tobolowsky (Sandy Ryerson), Romy Rosemont (Carole Hudson), Ben Bledsoe (Hank Saunders), Aaron Hendry (Darren), Justin Gaston

★ ★ ★

MUSIC, MUSIC, MUSIC!

Featured Music by the Original Artists:

"You Can Do It (Put Your Back into It)" – Ice Cube
"Shining Star" – Earth Wind & Fire
"Flight of the Bumblebee" – The Swingle Singers
"A Fifth of Beethoven" – The Swingle Singers
"Soul Bossa Nova" – The Swingle Singers
"Moonlight Sonata" – The Swingle Singers
"Golliwog's Cakewalk" – The Swingle Singers
"Chewing Gum" – Annie

★

Audition Songs for New Directions:

"Respect" by Otis Redding – sung by Mercedes Jones
"Mr Cellophane" from *Chicago* – sung by Kurt Hummel
"I Kissed a Girl" by Katy Perry – sung by Tina Cohen-Chang
"On My Own" from *Les Misérables* – sung by Rachel Berry

★

Shhhh! Secret Solos (songs sung in private):

"Can't Fight This Feeling" by Reo Speedwagon – Finn Hudson singing in the shower

★

Featured Performances:

"Where Is Love?" from *Oliver!* – sung by Hank Saunders and Sandy Ryerson
"Lovin', Touchin', Squeezin'" by Journey – sung by Finn Hudson and Darren
"Rehab" by Amy Winehouse – sung by Vocal Adrenaline
"That's the Way (I Like It)" by KC and the Sunshine Band – sung by McKinley's Glee Club (1993)
"(Shake, Shake, Shake) Shake Your Booty" by KC and the Sunshine Band – sung by McKinley's Glee Club (1993)

★

New Directions Performances:

"Sit Down, You're Rockin' the Boat" from *Guys and Dolls* (Practice Room)
"You're the One That I Want" from *Grease* (Practice Room)
"Don't Stop Believin'" by Journey (School Auditorium)

THE SCORE

★ ★ ★

William McKinley High School Spanish teacher Will Schuester, wants to resurrect the school's glee club to its former glory as National Champions. But he runs into a host of problems, including apathetic students, an over-achieving/over-bearing talented diva in the making, an unsupportive wife, a budget-crunched Principal and rival faculty member Sue Sylvester, who has no patience for anyone or anything trying to shift focus from her nationally recognized Cheerios cheerleading team. Despite the odds, he manages to cobble together an eclectic mix of talented misfits to form the New Directions glee club. Is this just a recipe for total disaster?

★

Mr. Schue's wife Terri is going to have a baby.

Mr. Schuester resurrects the glee club.

HIGHLIGHTS:

★ ★ ★

★ New Directions' awkward first attempt at choreography around Artie's wheelchair with "Sit Down You're Rockin' the Boat".

★ Emma Pillsbury's anti-germ lunch regiment, that involves gloves and sanitizing wipes.

★ Mr. Schuester scraping gum off of a smitten Emma's shoes so she doesn't have to.

★ Sue Sylvester's megaphone rants at her practising team.

★ Mr. Schue finding out that his wife Terri is going to have a baby.

★ New Directions performing an amazing rendition of "Don't Stop Believin'".

★

A WORD FROM PRINCIPAL FIGGINS

It's not easy running McKinley High, but as Principal Figgins has come to discover, it helps to have ground rules. Here are his secrets to keeping things under control:

 <u>DON'T</u> allow the student body to use the grounds as a urinal. It's a slippery slope to disaster.

 <u>DO</u> create ways to generate new funds. Maybe open the school as a meeting place for the alcoholically challenged? They might bring cookies?!

 <u>DO</u> keep parents happy at all times – that makes it easier to hide things from them day to day.

 <u>DO</u> save money on dry cleaning by staying domestic. Cleaned in the USA!

 <u>DO</u> remember to spell check the students' signs. Ignore that rule at your own peril.

 <u>DO</u> remember to enforce a dress code for school performances. No one wants to see anyone's junk at any time!

<u>DO</u> try to keep Sue Sylvester away from other faculty members, as it never ends well.

<u>DO</u> remember to tape your conversations with Sue Sylvester. She's wily!

<u>DO</u> pre-approve appropriate songs for school assemblies, otherwise there will be calls . . . oh yes, there will be calls.

 <u>NEVER</u> let Sue see you sweat, because her next move is to snap your neck when you look away.

Principal Figgins

It takes a special person to run William McKinley High School. And Principal Figgins really is that special.

Angry parents were up in arms at the school's performance of "Push It".

Principal Figgins would agree that it's tough at the top. Even though being responsible for the well-being and education of hundreds of teenagers all wrestling with their raging hormones for four years sounds like a job made in hell, taking care of the kids is actually the easy part. It's the backstage craziness that makes the job murder. But even with the constant budget cuts, temperamental school boards, angry parents and wacko employees with inflated God complexes, Principal Figgins manages to keep the Titans towering (even if his nerves suffer greatly for it). It's certainly more glamorous than being an actor on a Mumbai Air commercial . . . but that's just a dirty rumour!

But perhaps Figgins' biggest scandal is the war between two of his faculty members: Cheerios coach Sue Sylvester and Will Schuester, Spanish teacher/new show choir director. Figgins has catered to Sylvester's excessive demands (European uniform dry cleaning anyone?) because of her freakish work ethic and the McKinley Cheerios team's national acclaim. They're big news, so he's given them a big budget; at the expense of smaller clubs like glee . . . Although Will Schuester has agreed to fund glee for the meantime, Sue is scared. Any small success will see her budget cut in favour of them! So Sylvester sets out to bring down the gleeks.

To top it all, the school board and various parents were up in arms at New Directions' saucy and spunky first school performance of "Push It".

Ever since, it's been one thing after another, what with Sue blackmailing him over the sock commercial, Terri Schuester's terrible short tenure as school nurse, firing and then reinstating Mr. Schuester for a mattress commercial his glee kids shot, and finding out Sylvester helped rival schools cheat to attempt to beat New Directions at Sectionals.

It's enough to drive a lesser man to drink, but thank goodness for Principal Figgins it's just all in a day's work at McKinley High.

"SHOWMANCE"

Writer(s): Ryan Murphy, Brad Falchuk, Ian Brennan

Director: Ryan Murphy

Guest Stars: Valorie Hubbard (Peggy), Jennifer Aspen (Kendra)

★ ★ ★

MUSIC, MUSIC, MUSIC!

Featured Music by the Original Artists:

"Ain't That a Kick in the Head" – Dean Martin

★

Audition Songs for New Directions:

"I Say a Little Prayer" by Dionne Warwick, sung by Quinn Fabray, Brittany and Santana Lopez

★

Shhhh! Secret Solos (songs sung in private):

"All by Myself" by Eric Carmen – sung by Emma Pillsbury (Emma's Car)
"Take a Bow" by Rihanna – sung by Rachel Berry (Rachel's Bedroom)

★

New Directions Performances:

"Le Freak" by Chic (Practice Room)
"Gold Digger" by Kanye West featuring Jamie Foxx – lead vocal by Will Schuester (Practice Room)
"Push It" by Salt-N-Pepa (School Assembly)

Mr. Schuester sings "Gold Digger" by Kanye West.

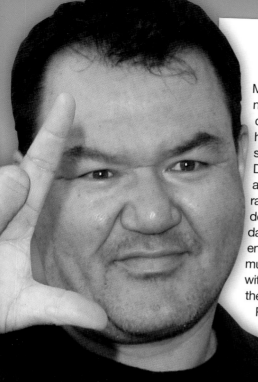

★ ★ ★ THE SCORE

Mr. Schuester discovers he needs 12 students to qualify to compete at Regionals, so he has to figure out how to draft seven more students into New Directions. Meanwhile, there's already dissention in the glee ranks as Rachel and the others don't agree with Mr. Schue's dated song selections. They end up committing a show mutiny when they come up with their own performance for the school assembly of Salt-N-Pepa's "Push It".

At home, Will is stressing out over Terri's desire to buy a new house for the baby, so he takes an after-hours janitorial job. At the doctor's, Terri finds out she is experiencing a hysterical pregnancy, but she decides to let Will think they're still having a baby.

Rachel and Finn discover they are attracted to each other and they have a cheeky kiss. However, Finn is loyal to his girlfriend Quinn, who decides to join glee club to keep an eye on him.

★

Coach Tanaka tries to ask Emma Pillsbury out on a date.

★ ★ ★ HIGHLIGHTS:

★ Will shows his rappin' skilz when he leads the students in Kanye's "Gold Digger".

★ Coach Tanaka's awkward attempt to ask Emma out on a date.

★ Rachel's blistering version of Rihanna's "Take a Bow".

★

Rachel rocks out with a awesome version of Rihanna's "Take a Bow."

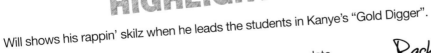

"ACAFELLAS"

Mercedes mistakes Kurt's friendship for romantic feelings.

Rachel talks the gleeks into enlisting the help of Dakota Stanley.

Writer: Ryan Murphy

Director: John S. Scott

Guest Stars: Josh Groban, Debra Monk (Mrs. Schuester), Victor Garber (Mr. Schuester), John Lloyd Young (Henri St. Pierre), Kent Avenido (Howard Bamboo), Whit Hertford (Dakota Stanley)

★ ★ ★

MUSIC, MUSIC, MUSIC!

Shhhh! Secret Solos (songs sung in private):

"Bust Your Windows" by Jazmine Sullivan – sung by Mercedes Jones and the Cheerios (Car Wash)

★ Presenting: The Acafellas!:

"For He's a Jolly Good Fellow" (Teachers' Lounge)
"This Is How We Do It" by Montell Jordan (Will's Living Room)
"Poison" by Bell Biv DeVoe (Local Bar)
"I Wanna Sex You Up" by Color Me Badd (School Auditorium)

★ Other Featured Performances:

"Mercy" by Duffy – sung by Vocal Adrenaline
"La Camisa Negra" by Juanes – danced to by Will Schuester, Finn Hudson and Noah Puckerman (Practice Room)

THE SCORE

Mr. Schue is so insulted when his glee singers diss his choreography skills that he decides to go out on his own and form an a cappella boy band, Acafellas, featuring Ken Tanaka, Henri St. Pierre, Howard Bamboo and the persistant Sandy Ryerson.

Meanwhile, Rachel enlists the help of Vocal Adrenaline's award-winning choreographer Dakota Stanley for their routine so they can compete at Regionals level.

Will's new confidence freaks out Terri, who's desperate to get pregnant to cover up her lie. Emma also sees the change and it makes her even more attracted to the forbidden fruit that is Will Schuester. And Mercedes mistakes Kurt's friendship for romantic feelings.

Will creates a cappella boy band — Acafellas.

HIGHLIGHTS:

★ Josh Groban showing up for the Acafellas' PTA performance.

★ Mercedes' jealousy-induced showstopper "Bust Your Windows".

★ Will's dad's encouraging talk about following your dreams.

★ Dakota Stanley's trashing of the gleeks.

MCKINLEY SLAM PAGE

OK, it's no secret that not all of the cliques get along at McKinley and sometimes the student body can get a little bitchy. After some well-placed burns, it's usually back to normal around here. All is forgiven . . . unless you write the best ones down!

MERCEDES:
I just want to get a record deal... and then I won't need to speak to anyone else.

KURT ON RACHEL:
Does Rachel think she's the queen? I think I missed that election...

QUINN ON FINN:
Urgh, ever since Finn joined New Directions, people think he's gay! And what does that make me?!

KURT ON RACHEL:
I'd like to give Rachel a make-over. Everyone knows I dress better than her - she has terrible style.

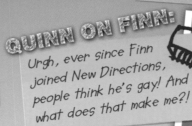

PUCK ON FINN:
The dude can't dance!

KURT ABOUT BRITTANY:
If Finn's going to cheat, why on earth would he cheat off her?

ARTIE ON RACHEL:
Dramatic, much? No one even notices when she storms out of rehearsals any more.

PUCK ON RACHEL:
She is SO annoying, but she sure can sing!

BRITTANY ON RACHEL:
I don't want to be in a picture with her. That picture will get totally destroyed . . . by me!

ARTIE ON RACHEL:
Well, she's irritating most of the time, but we don't take that personally.

THE WRATH OF SUE SYLVESTER

If there's one thing you want to do at all costs at McKinley High, it's stay on Sue Sylvester's good side. However, if you manage to make Sue mad . . . run!

Here's a cheat sheet on how to keep yourself in Sue's good books:

SUE SYLVESTER CHEAT SHEET

<u>NEVER</u> bring up how hard practice is, or she'll start talking about her Baywatch audition . . . again.

<u>DON'T</u> get pregnant - she hates that.

<u>DON'T</u> bore her.

<u>DON'T</u> cry in front of her, unless you are in pain . . . then go ahead.

<u>DO</u> appreciate her time and attention towards making your life miserable.

<u>DON'T</u> make things personal or she'll ruin you with an almost religious devotion.

<u>DO</u> show terror when she approaches. She appreciates your drool and uncontrollable shaking.

<u>DO</u> yell at a homeless person when she's near. It's like reading a Christmas card to her.

<u>DO</u> wear extra deodorant. The smell of your fear only sets her off.

<u>DON'T</u> try to produce an elementary school version of Hair. She just might throw up on you in disgust.

<u>DON'T</u> show her that she's gotten to you. She breathes your frustration in like freshly made brownies.

<u>DON'T</u> try to bring down Sue Sylvester - that only gives her a good reason to get up in the morning.

"PREGGERS"

Writer: Brad Falchuk

Director: Brad Falchuk

Guest Stars: Kurt Fuller (Mr. McClung), Bill A. Jones (Rod Remington), Mike O'Malley (Burt Hummel)

★ ★ ★

MUSIC, MUSIC, MUSIC!

Featured Music by the Original Artists:

"Single Ladies (Put a Ring on It)" by Beyoncé Knowles – danced to by Kurt Hummel, Brittany and Tina Cohen-Chang (Kurt's Basement) and danced to by Kurt with the McKinley Titans Football Team (Football Field)

★

Audition Songs for the High School Musical, Cabaret:

"Taking Chances" by Celine Dion – sung by Rachel Berry (School Auditorium)

★

New Directions Performances:

"Tonight" from *West Side Story* – sung by Tina Cohen-Chang (School Auditorium)

Beyoncé provides the dance track.

Tina sings a musical classic, "Tonight".

★ ★ ★ THE SCORE

Worried his father isn't proud of his effeminate ways, Kurt decides to "audition" as kicker for the McKinley High Titans football team. It turns out that Kurt's unusual kicking, rhythmically styled to Beyoncé's tune "Single Ladies" inspires the ever-losing team to get in touch with their own inner boogie.

At glee practice, Will gives Tina the solo for the *West Side Story* number, which enrages Rachel and spurs her to quit. Sue blackmails Principal Figgins to let her hire back Sandy Ryerson in the hope that he will lure Rachel into the school musical and away from glee permanently.

Quinn tells Finn that she's pregnant with his baby, even though she knows that Puck is the father. Terri enlists her sister Kendra's help in lying to Will about the baby. She finds out about Quinn's secret pregnancy and corners the girl to hatch a very cunning plan.

Sue Sylvester's first appearance on "Sue's Corner".

★ ★ ★ HIGHLIGHTS:

★ Figgins' Mumbai Air anti-clotting stockings commercial.

★ The football team's on-field dance routine to "Single Ladies".

★ Kurt admitting to his dad that he's gay and Burt's touching response.

★ Sue Sylvester's first appearance on "Sue's Corner".

★

Writer: Ian Brennan

Director: John Scott

Guest Stars: Kristin Chenoweth (April Rhodes), Jayson Blair (Chris), Susan Leslie (Sandra)

★ ★ ★

MUSIC, MUSIC, MUSIC!

Featured Music by the Original Artists:

"I Want a New Drug" by Huey Lewis and the News (Bowling Alley)

★

Featured Performances:

"Maybe This Time" from *Cabaret* – sung by April Rhodes and Rachel Berry (Practice Room)
"Cabaret" from *Cabaret* – sung by Rachel Berry (Music Room)
"Alone" by Heart – sung by April Rhodes and Will Schuester (Bowling Alley Bar)

★

New Directions Performances:

"Don't Stop Believin'" by Journey – leads sung by Finn Hudson and Quinn Fabray (Practice Room)
"Last Name" by Carrie Underwood – lead sung by April Rhodes (School Auditorium)
"Somebody to Love" by Queen – leads sung by Rachel Berry and Finn Hudson (School Auditorium)

Rachel sings "Cabaret" in the Music Room.

TAKEN"

Desperate to up New Directions' game, Mr. Schue manages to track down the former McKinley glee star April Rhodes. He finds out that she's an alcoholic down on her luck, so he offers to help her finally graduate high school if she joins glee. April agrees and impresses everyone with her talent, but not with her bad influence on the singers.

Rachel and Mr. Ryerson clash as they rehearse for *Cabaret*, which makes her re-think her decision to leave show choir. Worried that glee club will fold without Rachel's talent, Finn decides to woo her back by taking her on a date. Just as Rachel decides to return, Puck announces that Quinn is pregnant. The news devastates Rachel but she decides to return just in time to give an amazing performance of "Somebody to Love".

Kurt gets drunk and pukes on Ms. Pillsbury's shoes.

★ ★ ★
HIGHLIGHTS:

★ A drunk Kurt puking on Ms. Pillsbury's shoes.

★ April's awesome renditions of "Alone" with Mr. Schue and then "Last Name" with the gleeks.

★ Rachel realizing her selfish ways and returning to the group.

★ April deciding her life is a train wreck and leaving McKinley with a new goal to straighten out her life.

★

Finn decides to woo Rachel to save glee club.

WILLIAM McKINLEY HIGH SCHOOL
SLUSHIE HALL OF SHAME

If you attend McKinley High, you know exactly where you sit on the social ladder based on how many slushies you've taken to the face. Are you icy facial free? Then you must be part of the popular elite. Do you always have an extra set of clothes waiting in your locker? Well, then chances are that you spend a lot of your Friday nights alone at home . . . or maybe you're just in glee club.

With the launch of New Directions this year, the slushies were flying fast and furious in the halls and there were some truly stunning hits to savour:

A great way to hide from those slushies!

SLUSHIED

Rachel Berry gets hit with a cherry slushie by Puck next to the glee sign-up board. ("Pilot")

SLUSHIED

For the first time ever, Finn Hudson gets a slushie to the face by Dave Karofsky. It's grape. ("Mash-Up")

DOUBLE SLUSHIED

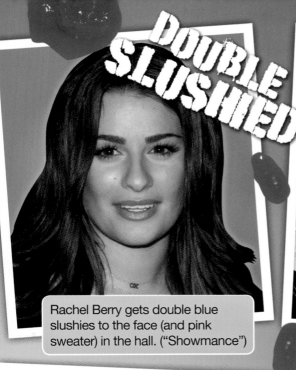

MEGA SLUSHIED

Rachel Berry gets double blue slushies to the face (and pink sweater) in the hall. ("Showmance")

Five football players give Finn and Quinn an epic dousing together. ("Mash-Up")

SLUSHIED

Kurt takes one for the team and slushies himself to save Finn from a beating. ("Mash-Up")

DOUBLE SLUSHIED

Puck takes a slushie when he steps out in the hallways with Rachel on his arm. ("Mash-Up")

SLUSHIE SHOWER

The glee club gives Mr. Schue a massive slushie shower to make him a true gleek. ("Mash-Up")

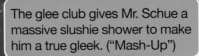

Writer: Ryan Murphy
Director: Elodie Keene
Guest Stars: Joe Hursley (Joe)

★ ★ ★

MUSIC, MUSIC, MUSIC!

Featured Music by the Original Artists:

"Break My Stride" by Matthew Wilder

★

New Directions Performances:

"It's My Life"/"Confessions Part II" by Bon Jovi & Usher –
sung by the men of New Directions (Practice Room)
"Halo"/"Walking on Sunshine" by Beyoncé Knowles & Katrina and the Waves –
lead sung by Rachel Berry and the ladies of New Directions (Practice Room)

THE SCORE

Disturbed by his singers' relaxed attitude towards preparing for Sectionals, Will decides to shake things up by pitting the boys against the girls in a mash-up competition to see who prevails.

Sue panics that the glee club's bonding and Quinn's pregnancy will cost the Cheerios their National title. She decides it's time to get personal and alerts Terri to Will's dangerous flirtation with Emma Pillsbury.

Sue recruits Terri as the school nurse so she can keep closer tabs on her husband.

The kids find themselves completley exhausted with so many personal and school commitments so they visit Terri, who provides them with vitamin supplements that end up being uppers.

Principal Figgins figures out the truth, dismisses Terri and then appoints Sue as co-director of glee club with Will.

Emma asks Will why she shouldn't marry Ken.

Sue is appointed co-director of glee club with Will. Uh-oh . . .

Sue's diary must be a scary read.

Bon Jovi inspired the men of New Directions with "It's My Life".

HIGHLIGHTS:

★ Sue's dear diary moments filled with her evil (and hilarious) plans.

★ Ken's awkward, honest and heartfelt proposal to Emma Pillsbury.

★ Emma asking Will for any reason why she shouldn't marry Ken.

★ Sue's look when she's given control over glee club.

episode "THROWDOWN"

Writer: Brad Falchuk

Director: Ryan Murphy

Guest Stars: Kenneth Choi (Dr. Wu), Amy Hill (Dr. Chin), Jennifer Jean Snyder (Reporter)

★ ★ ★

MUSIC, MUSIC, MUSIC!

Featured Music by the Original Artists:

"O Fortuna" from *Carmina Burana*

★

Featured Performances:

"You Keep Me Hangin' On" by The Supremes –
sung by Quinn Fabray and the Cheerios
(Football Field & School Auditorium)

★

New Directions Performances:

"Hate on Me" by Jill Scott – lead sung by Mercedes Jones, Sue's Elite Singers (Practice Room)
"Ride Wit' Me" by Nelly featuring City Spud – sung a cappella (Practice Room)
"No Air" by Jordin Sparks & Chris Brown – leads sung by Rachel Berry and Finn Hudson (Practice Room)
"Keep Holding On" by Avril Lavigne – leads sung by Rachel Berry and Finn Hudson (School Auditorium)

★ ★ ★

THE SCORE

Sue throws around her new power over glee club by separating the students into two groups: Sue's elite, which consists of all the minority kids, and the rest in Will's group. Her plan is to create a wedge amongst the choir singers so the club implodes. Will figures out her plan and fails her Cheerios in Spanish so they can't cheer.

Will takes Finn and Quinn to their very first ultrasound appointment after which he pushes Terri to allow him to be more involved in their own pregnancy. She arranges a fake appointment with her doctor, using Quinn's ultrasound images as her own.

Rachel and Quinn come to an uneasy truce over their feelings for Finn.

Sue loves her new power.

62

Mercedes rocks "Hate on Me".

There's no denying the chemistry between Rachel and Finn as they sing "No Air".

HIGHLIGHTS:

★ Mercedes' tour de force performance of "Hate on Me".

★ Will and Sue's slow-motion scream fest.

★ The look on Will's face when he thinks he is seeing his child for the first time.

★ The sizzling chemistry between Rachel and Finn during "No Air".

glee

episode "MASH-UP"

Writer: Ian Brennan

Director: Elodie Keene

Guest Star: Gina Hecht (Mrs. Puckerman)

MUSIC, MUSIC, MUSIC!

Featured Music by the Original Artists:

"Flight of the Bumblebee" – The Swingle Singers

★

Featured Performances:

"Thong Song" by Sisqó – sung by Will Schuester (Empty Classroom)
"What a Girl Wants" by Christina Aguilera – sung by Rachel Berry, played by Puck (Rachel's Bedroom)
"Sing, Sing, Sing" by Louis Prima – danced by Sue Sylvester and Will Schuester (Practice Room)
"I Could Have Danced All Night" from *My Fair Lady* – sung by Emma Pillsbury (Bridal Shop)

★

New Directions Performances:

"Bust a Move" by Young MC – lead sung by Will Schuester (Practice Room)
"Sweet Caroline" by Neil Diamond – lead sung and played by Noah Puckerman (Practice Room)

THE SCORE

Quinn and Finn face the cold, hard truth that their involvement with glee club has ruined their popularity status as they become victims of a slushie attack. The football team then decides that Finn isn't fit to be captain of the team any more and he's got to choose . . . it's going to be between them or glee.

Emma asks Will for dance lessons in preparation for her wedding to Ken. Meanwhile, Sue becomes a new person when she falls in love with the local news anchor.

Frustrated with Quinn, Puck decides to go after Rachel and they become a couple.

HIGHLIGHTS:

★ Sue's joyous (and shocking) dance with Will Schuester.

★ Puck not throwing a slushie in Rachel's face and her reaction.

★ Puck and Rachel's snogging session.

★ The ramped-up slushie wars that culminate in Kurt taking one for the team.

★ Puck singing "Sweet Caroline" to Rachel (and Quinn).

★ Sue Sylvester in a zoot suit!

★ Will's gleek slushie shower from the kids.

Will and Sue . . .
dance partners
made in heaven?!

OH BABY!

Psst... Fellow Titans, I don't need to tell you that it's been kind of crazy around McKinley this year. Maybe the most nutso is all the shocking baby mumma drama going on with the students and the teachers. Something must be in the water (or Sue Sylvester's locked desk drawers!) but luckily for us, nothing's remained a secret for long. In case you haven't been following along at home, here's a super-quick review of the hottest and most scandalous news:

Scandal #1

QUINN FABRAY CHEATS ON CELIBACY CLUB

The Cheerio queen's pious act wasn't fooling anyone, except maybe her parents and her dopey boyfriend Finn Hudson. Sure she preached abstinence and chastity, but we know someone who saw her and that love rat Puck getting frisky behind the football stands months ago!

Scandal #2

QUINN FABRAY CHEATS ON FINN HUDSON

If we were friends with Finn, we'd be happy to tell him "toldja so!" Quinn wasn't called Sue Sylvester's protégée for nothing! Finn's too much of a boy scout for fiery Quinn; she needs more of a jock superhero (hello, Puck!). And then when Finn joined glee . . . well, we knew that was the last straw with those two.

Cheater

Scandal #3

QUINN PREGNANT . . . BY NOAH PUCKERMAN!

Talk about being a cautionary tale! In less than a year, diva Quinn has lost her popularity, joined glee (come on!), been kicked out of the Cheerios and her house all because of a one-night fling with Noah Puckerman. OK, don't get us wrong, he's hot with a capital H-O-T, but man, no single night of passion is worth that fall from grace, sweetie!

Scandal #4

TERRI SCHUESTER GETS PREGNANT . . . SORT OF?

OK, so teacher gossip is usually B-O-R-I-N-G, but the Schuesters must have gone crazy this year or something (we told you glee was no good!) because those two are full of secrets. Now, we only know about this tasty bit of dirt because Mrs. Schue worked as our school nurse for like a minute. It turns out the two (who've been together for a zillion years) were trying to have a baby and they finally got lucky . . . or so he thought. While she was nursing us, she certainly looked preggo but it turns out she wasn't!

A friend of a friend's mum works at Mrs. Schue's doctor's office and she said she heard that Mrs. Schue and her nutty sister threatened Dr. Wu with a wacko lawsuit if he didn't lie and say her hysterical pregnancy was actually a real pregnancy to Mr. Schue. Crazers!

TERRI SCHUESTER BECOMES MCKINLEY'S SCHOOL NURSE . . . AND PILL PUSHER!

Most of us didn't think much of it when Mr. Schue's wife Terri got hired as our new school nurse. But she was pretty cool to talk to and she gave out these rad vitamin D pills that totally boosted our energy (I wrote a ten-page

paper in like, 20 minutes!). Of course, most good things are too good to be true and we soon found out those vitamins weren't vitamins at all and Mrs. Schue had no medical training. She only ever worked at Sheets-N-Things!

MR. SCHUE FINDS OUT MRS. SCHUESTER WAS NEVER PREGNANT

This is pretty sad actually. Between New Dorkrections . . . er, Directions and news of his baby, Mr. Schue was walking on sunshine for a couple months. He was really ecstatic but then we heard (around the time he got fired before Sectionals) that his whole world fell apart

at home. A kid who lives in his neighbourhood said Mr. Schue found a fake padded belly in his wife's drawer and when he confronted her about it – she finally admitted she wasn't preggo at all. Pretty evil, if you ask me.

Pill pusher

Yuck! Mr. Schue and Ms. Pillsbury are dating!

MR. AND MRS. SCHUESTER SEPARATE . . . AND NOW HE'S DATING MS. PILLSBURY!

OK, let me start by saying old people dating is just gross. When I heard Coach Tanaka was going out with Ms. Pillsbury, I totally threw up a little in my mouth. But then it was kinda sad when we heard Mr. Schue and Mrs. Schue were separated; we all felt awful for him about the

baby and being lied to like that. But then, like a week later, we heard rumours that he and Ms. Pillsbury were secretly dating. Get out! And eww!

glee cast

Emma Pillsbury

There ain't no dirt on this lady!

With her tiny frame, doe eyes and crisp, twee wardrobe, McKinley's guidance counsellor, Ms. Pillsbury flits about like the fairy princess of good advice. Just don't ask her to touch anything gross, unsanitary, or at all unhygienic. She has a bad case of mysophobia (or germophobia to you and me). She knows that she takes the cleaning thing a bit far, but it all stems from her brother and that incident at the dairy farm when they were little kids.

Regardless of her quirky phobias, no one questions Emma's love and dedication to the kids at McKinley High. She will always make time to provide advice on everything from cool sunglasses to future career plans. Matter of fact, there's nothing that she loves more, except maybe Will Schuester.

Emma has nursed a healthy crush on her fellow teacher for ages, but has never crossed any boundaries because he's a married man. However, things start to change when Will takes over glee club. His marriage starts to crack and Emma makes her shoulder free for Will until their bond gets too dangerous. Emma then flees into the arms of Coach Ken Tanaka.

Of course, the love quadrangle can't survive and everything comes apart for both couples in time for Sectionals. With Will's marriage busted and the lovely Emma's engagement to poor Ken in ruins – what will the future hold for this star-crossed pair?

She's so squeaky clean!

Jayma Mays

A small town girl with her sights set on the stars.

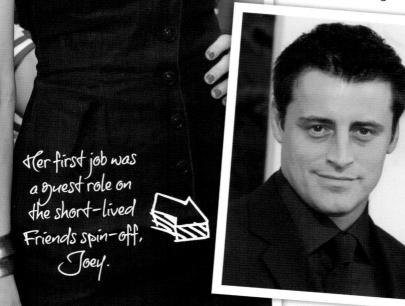

Born and raised in the western Virginian town, Grundy, Jayma Mays lived a traditionally suburban childhood dabbling in a variety of interests from singing to mathematics. She stayed in state for her college, attending Radford University, where she graduated with a degree in Performing Arts.

Not long after, Jayma made the leap to the west coast, auditioning for television and film roles. Her first job was a guest role on the short-lived *Friends* spin-off, *Joey*. She got her first film role in the thriller *Red Eye*. In the ensuing years, she worked steadily appearing in *House, Entourage, Epic Movie* and *Pushing Daisies*.

Two of her most recognized television roles were playing recurring characters named Charlie: one on *Ugly Betty* and the other as Masi Oka's love interest in the superhero drama *Heroes*. On film, she scored a big hit in the 2009 comedy *Paul Blart: Mall Cop*. But it wasn't until Ryan Murphy needed to cast a germophobic guidance counsellor in *Glee* that Jayma landed her first cast role as the sweet but slightly neurotic Emma Pillsbury.

In her personal life, Jayma is happily married to British actor Adam Campbell whom she met on the set of *Epic Movie*.

Her first job was a guest role on the short-lived Friends spin-off, Joey.

73

Writer: Ryan Murphy

Director: Paris Barclay

Guest Stars: Lauren Potter (Becky Jackson), Cheryl Francis Harrington (Nurse), Jeff Lewis (Manager), Robin Trocki (Jean Sylvester)

★ ★ ★

MUSIC, MUSIC, MUSIC!

Featured Music by the Original Artists:

"Dancing with Myself" by Billy Idol

★

Shhhh! Secret Solos (songs sung in private or internally):

"Dancing with Myself" by Billy Idol – sung by Artie Abrams (School Halls & Auditorium)

★

Featured Performances:

"Defying Gravity" from *Wicked* – co-leads sung by Rachel Berry and Kurt Hummel (Practice Room)

★

New Directions Performances:

"Proud Mary" by Ike and Tina Turner – leads sung by Mercedes Jones and Artie Abrams (School Auditorium)

★ ★ ★

THE SCORE

Money troubles hit everyone. Will lets the club know they need to raise funds so they can get a bus with handicap accessibility for Artie's wheelchair. However, the kids aren't very supportive about the problem or having a bake sale to raise funds the old-fashioned way. Finn promises Quinn he will find a way to pay for their escalating medical bills. Puck offers Quinn financial support. Puck's proximity to Quinn incites jealousy in both guys and they get into a fight.

Kurt decides that he wants to challenge gutsy Rachel for the lead vocals to "Defying Gravity". But as prank calls start to come to the house referring to his sexuality, Kurt decides to re-think his course of action to save his father embarrassment.

Figgins tells Sue to hold auditions for poor Quinn's now free slot on the Cheerios team.

Who's got the gravity voice?

★ ★ ★ HIGHLIGHTS:

★ Kurt and Rachel's vocal-defying sing-off.

★ The all-wheelchair version of "Proud Mary".

★ Sue's wonderfully revealing and tender visit to her sister with Down's syndrome.

★

"BALLAD"

Finn sings to his baby's sonogram.

Quinn's parents are shocked at her baby news.

Writer: Brad Falchuk

Director: Brad Falchuk

Guest Stars: Sarah Drew (Suzy Pepper), Gregg Henry (Russell Fabray),
Charlotte Ross (Judy Fabray), J. R. Nutt (Edgar Newdle)

★ ★ ★

MUSIC, MUSIC, MUSIC!

Featured Music by the Original Artists:

"More Than Words" by Extreme

★

Featured Performances:

"Endless Love" by Lionel Richie & Diana Ross – sung by Rachel Berry and Will Schuester (Practice Room)
"I'll Stand by You" by The Pretenders – sung by Finn Hudson (School Auditorium)
"Don't Stand So Close to Me"/"Young Girl" by The Police & Gary Puckett & The Union Gap –
sung by Will Schuester (Practice Room)
"Crush" by Jennifer Paige – sung by Rachel Berry (Mr. Schuester's Car)
"(You're) Having My Baby" by Paul Anka – sung by Finn Hudson (The Fabray Dining Room)

★

New Directions Performances:

"Lean on Me" by Bill Withers – lead sung by Artie Abrams (Practice Room)

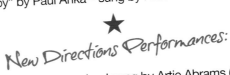

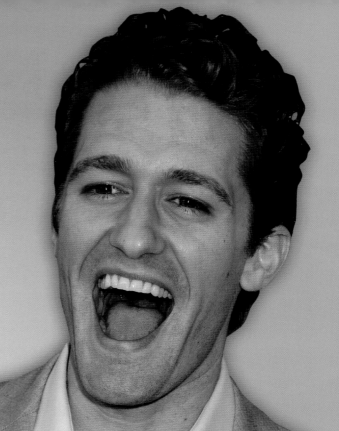

THE SCORE

Will challenges all the singers to explore their emotional sides by selecting and singing ballads to one another. He splits the singers into pairs and they have to find the perfect songs to reveal themselves. Rachel finds herself developing a massive crush on Mr. Schue, which makes him very uncomfortable. Kurt is nursing his own crush on Finn, who he hopes to bond with as they work to select their ballads. Puck confesses to Mercedes that he's the father of Quinn's baby. Now that's scandalous!

★

Mr. Schue better watch out for crazy student Suzy Pepper.

HIGHLIGHTS:

★ The sad and wacky tale of the other student who was obsessed with Will – Suzy Pepper.

★ Kurt and Finn bonding over their lives and how to express themselves.

★ Finn's stirring performance of "I'll Stand by You" to his baby's sonogram.

★ Will's mash-up song that makes both Emma and Rachel swoon over him.

★ Finn's emotional confession to his mother about the baby.

★ Quinn's parents' shock at her baby news and the sad outcome.

★

McKINLEY

In love, out of love, or just swooning from afar – there's a whole lot of chemistry going on in the halls of McKinley High. Keep track of all the important connections and broken hearts:

FACULTY HEARTS

In love with Rod Remington co-anchor of the WOHN TV news (he broke her heart)

Married to Terri Schuester (now separated)

Attracted to Emma Pillsbury (now dating)

Rachel Berry had a crush on Mr. Schue

Engaged to Ken Tanaka (now broken up)

STUDENT AFFAIRS

Briefly dated Noah "Puck" Puckerman

Attracted to and had a fling with Noah "Puck" Puckerman

Has a huge crush on Finn Hudson (kissed)

Boyfriend of Quinn Fabray – thought he was her baby-daddy (broken up)

Girlfriend of Finn Hudson – lied to him about being pregnant with his child (broken up)

ROMANCES

Had flirty texts with Santana

Had flirty texts with Brittany

Attracted to Quinn Fabray – got her pregnant.

Briefly dated Rachel Berry

Has a creepy crush on Rachel Berry

Had a crush on Tina Cohen-Chang

Maintains her crush on Artie Abrams

Had a crush on Kurt Hummel (now BFFs)

Has a huge crush on Finn Hudson

Had an obsessive crush on Mr. Schue

Writer: Ian Brennan

Director: Bill D'Elia

Guest Stars: Eve (Grace Hitchens), Michael Hitchcock (Dalton Rumba), Dawn Noel Pignuola (Jayelle), Telisha Shaw (Aphasia)

★ ★ ★

MUSIC, MUSIC, MUSIC!

Featured Performances:

"Bootylicious" by Destiny's Child – sung by Jane Addams Girls Choir (School Auditorium)
"Don't Make Me Over" by Dionne Warwick – instrumental underscore, sung by Mercedes Jones (School Hallways)
"You're the One That I Want" from *Grease* – sung by Finn Hudson and Rachel Berry (Rachel's Bedroom)
"Papa Don't Preach" by Madonna – sung by Quinn Fabray (Will Schuester's Living Room)

★

New Directions Performances:

"Hair"/"Crazy" in Love" from *Hair* & Beyoncé featuring Jay-Z (Practice Room)
"Imagine" by John Lennon – duet with Haverbrook Deaf Choir (Practice Room)
"True Colours" by Cyndi Lauper – lead sung by Tina Cohen-Chang (School Auditorium)

Rachel sings Dionne Warwick.

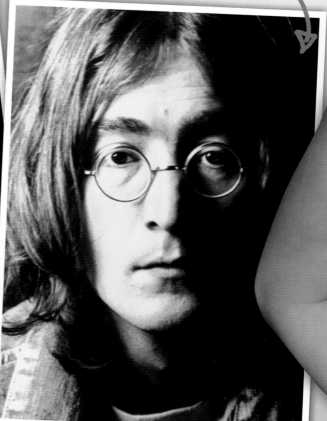

Sue sets in motion her latest plan to destroy glee club – find out what the group's Sectionals playlist is so she can pass it on to the other competing schools. Cunning Will soon figures out she's up to something so he decides to check out the competition rivals on his own. He asks both schools to perform friendly scrimmages at McKinley.

Quinn starts to question who would be a better father to her unborn baby. Meanwhile Terri's baby ruse is getting harder to keep from Will, especially when Quinn decides to keep her baby.

Kurt offers to give Rachel a makeover so she can woo Finn; a diabolical plan on Kurt's part because he knows Finn prefers girls with natural beauty.

★

Rachel attempts to seduce Finn.

★ ★ ★
HIGHLIGHTS:

★ Jane Addams Academy's performance of "Bootylicious".

★ Quinn and Puck perfecting babysitting through a song together.

★ Haverbrook's rendition of "Imagine" with New Directions as back-up.

★ Rachel's pathetic attempt at a Sandy-like seduction of Finn, à la *Grease*.

★ Kurt's honest appraisal of what people really think of Rachel.

★

Rachel is inspired by Sandy from Grease.

"MATTRESS"

Writer: Ryan Murphy

Director: Elodie Keene

Guest Stars: John Ross Bowie (Dennis), Chuck Spitler (Randy Cusperberg)

★ ★ ★

MUSIC, MUSIC, MUSIC!

Featured Music by the Original Artists:

"All I Want Is You" by The Cars

★

Featured Performances:

"Smile" by Lily Allen – sung by Rachel Berry and Finn Hudson (Practice Room)

★

Shhhh! Secret Solos (songs sung in private or internally):

"Smile" by Charlie Chaplin – sung by Rachel Berry (Yearbook Photo Shoot)

★

New Directions Performances:

"Jump" by Van Halen (Mattress Land Store)

"Smile" by Charlie Chaplin (Montage underscore)

★ ★ ★

THE SCORE

Emma and Ken's wedding is fast approaching and the coach draws a line in the sand for his fiancée's loyalty by setting the reception at the same time as Sectionals.

The yearbook photographer sets up but Will is informed by Figgins that there's no space for New Directions unless he can come up with $1,000 to pay for the page. Meanwhile, most of the glee kids don't want to be in the picture because the popular kids always deface the library's copy of the glee club yearbook page. Only Rachel wants a picture and she compromises with Will for a quarter page that will fit two glee members.

Rachel stumbles on an opportunity to pay for the page by enlisting the glee club to star in a local mattress store commercial. When Sue sees the commercial, she finds a way to get the glee club disqualified. However, Will takes the blame and offers to give up glee so they can still perform. Emma is made director.

Will stumbles upon Terri's fake baby padding and makes her confess her terrible secret. He walks out on her.

Will finally
learns the truth
from Terri.

★ ★ ★
HIGHLIGHTS:

★ The group's rendition of Charlie Chaplin's bittersweet "Smile".

★ Quinn standing up to Sue about her hypocrisy and getting back into the Cheerios.

★ The New Directions kids all getting together to pose for their picture.

★ Will finally learning the truth from Terri and the devastation on his face.

★

SECTIONAL RIVALS

HAVERFORD SCHOOL FOR THE DEAF
DAYTON, OHIO

Show Choir Director:
Dalton Rumba

Haverford, a school for hearing-impaired kids put together a show choir group featuring deaf students that sign their performance with the music. Their heartfelt and graceful performance style quickly sways audience sentiment in their favour during competitions, which makes them extremely tough competitors and worthy opponents.

JANE ADDAMS ACADEMY
FEMALE JUVENILE HALL HALFWAY HOUSE

Show Choir Director:
Grace Hitchens

The all-female student body of Jane Addams Academy is made up of teens trying to overcome their broken pasts to start anew. Perhaps more street smart than members of the other peer choirs, the Jane Addams ladies make it clear from their first moments on the stage that they aren't afraid to get in your face with their musical song stylings. Winning Sectionals for them isn't just a trophy but a possible ticket to a better life for themselves.

WESTERN OHIO HIGH SCHOOL SHOW CHOIR SECTIONALS

BUCKEYE CIVIC AUDITORIUM

Sectionals Competition Playlists

JANE ADDAMS ACADEMY

"And I Am Telling You I'm Not Going" from *Dreamgirls*

"Proud Mary" by Ike and Tina Turner

★ ★ ★ ★ ★ ★

HAVERFORD SCHOOL FOR THE DEAF
DAYTON, OHIO

"Don't Stop Believin'" by Journey

★ ★ ★ ★ ★ ★

WILLIAM MCKINLEY HIGH SCHOOL'S NEW DIRECTIONS

"Don't Rain on My Parade" from *Funny Girl*

"You Can't Always Get What You Want" by the Rolling Stones

★ ★ ★ ★ ★

Official Judges:

Candace Dystra
5th Runner-up, Miss Ohio 2005

Rod Remington
Co-anchor, WOHN TV

Donna Landries
Ohio State Vice Comptroller

★ ★ ★ ★ ★

Grace Hitchens goes for the trophy with Jane Addams Academy.

Steve Perry from Journey.

Some of New Directions.

Writer: Brad Falchuk

Director: Brad Falchuk

Guest Stars: Eve (Grace Hitchens), Anna Camp (Candace Dystra), Peter Choi (Emcee), Patricia Forte (Donna Landries), Bill A. Jones (Rod Remington), Thomasina Gross (Perfect Engleberger) Michael Hitchcock (Dalton Rumba),

★ ★ ★

Featured Performances:

"And I Am Telling You I'm Not Going" from *Dreamgirls* – sung by Mercedes Jones (Practice Room)

★

New Directions Performances:

"My Life Would Suck Without You" by Kelly Clarkson – lead sung by Rachel Berry (Practice Room)

★ ★ ★

THE SCORE

Sectionals are here but everything is a mess. The singers have to come up with their own playlist without Mr. Schue's help. Rachel spills the truth about Quinn's baby to Finn and it sends him reeling so badly that he quits glee club. At Sectionals, the team discovers the competition has plundered their playlist in a desperate attempt to win. Rachel and the singers scramble to create a new set list when Finn arrives with a show-stopping number and forgiveness for his fellow gleeks. New Directions performs beautifully and win Sectionals.

Will arrives at Emma and Ken's wedding but it's been called off.

She finally admits her feelings for him and he attempts to kiss her after he reveals that he's left Terri. Emma walks away and resigns from McKinley.

Figgins finds out what Sue did to bring down the glee club and he suspends her.

In a tense, and heart-stopping finalé Will stops Emma with a kiss before she leaves for ever.

Finn saves the show.

★

Guess who got suspended?

HIGHLIGHTS:

★ The gleeks sing "My Life Would Suck Without You" to thank Mr. Schue.

★ Rachel's goose-bump-inducing version of "Don't Rain on My Parade".

★ Will and Emma's first kiss!

★ Sue finally getting her comeuppance.

★ Sue and Will squaring off again with the promise of future fireworks when she returns.

★

GRACE HITCHENS
(EVE)
JANE ADDAMS ACADEMY

As director of the Jane Addams Academy show choir, Grace Hitchens has always had an uphill battle. A half-way house for juvenile girls with troubled pasts, the Academy has the challenge of trying to correct the bad patterns of young women who grew up without the benefit of family or directional support. Through show choir, Hitchens tries to direct their restless energy into song and dance. When Will Schuester makes a trip to the Academy to scope the competition out, he is moved by how Hitchens is doing so much with so little. He invites Grace and her team to McKinley to perform, which they do rather impressively, and provocatively, with Destiny's Child's "Bootylicious". Turns out Hitchens has taught her girls the magic of "hairography", or twirling and shaking one's hair to distract from any vocal or dancing shortcomings.

A street-smart educator, Grace knows she has to do everything she can to give her girls a leg-up because the difference between winning and losing for them could mean their very future. So when Sue Sylvester offers her New Directions' Sectionals playlist ahead of the competition, Grace takes it and uses two of the songs for their own performance. Sure it's dirty, low-down cheating, but in Grace's mind it's all for her girls. That is, until McKinley's Emma Pillsbury calls Grace out at Sectionals and reminds her that not only is it dishonest, but it also dishonours the true talents of the Jane Addams girls.

A street-smart educator.

When laid out like that, Grace realized the error in her judgement and planned to confess to the Sectional judges. However, it was too late and New Directions were named the winners anyway. But that didn't stop Grace from confessing to Principal Figgins, which resulted in Sue Sylvester's suspension - some real justice in the end.

SPOTLIGHT

DALTON RUMBA
(MICHAEL HITCHCOCK)
HAVERFORD SCHOOL FOR THE DEAF
DAYTON, OHIO

The uptight director of the Haverford show choir, Dalton Rumba is another glee leader dealing with the challenges of his student body. In his case, it's finding a way for deaf or hearing-impaired students to express themselves dynamically through song. Plus, it doesn't help that Rumba is also deaf in one ear from a case of scarlet fever as a youth.

Protective of his students, he's developed a bit of a chip on his shoulder on their behalf against the hearing world. He's quick to cite prejudice in others against his students when a situation doesn't go his way.

He gets very offended when Will Schuester welcomes the Jane Adams Academy show choir to McKinley but not his Haverbrook students. Embarrassed, Will invites them too, which results in a moving duet between the schools to John Lennon's "Imagine".

However, that doesn't settle the bad blood between Rumba and Schuester, which makes the Haverford director vulnerable to Sue Sylvester's offer of the New Directions' Sectional playlist. Unlike Grace, Dalton doesn't suffer any guilt from their cheating and at Sectionals is even celebratory about getting one up on McKinley. He is unapologetic when his team uses "Don't Stop Believin'" at the competition, and flaunts it in Emma Pillsbury's face. However, sometime after their performance, Rumba finally decides to do right and, with Grace Hitchens, confesses to McKinley's Principal Figgins.

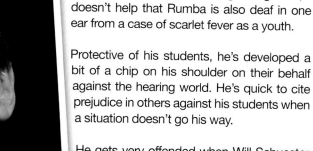

Dalton Rumba has his students' best interests at heart and he's prepared to do anything to protect them.

YEARBOOK AWARDS

The McKinley kids have cast their vote and here are the awards for this year's "most likely..."

McKINLEY'S "MOST LIKELY..."

Most likely to still get ID'd when they're 30 –
Kurt Hummel

Best cupcake recipe –
Noah "Puck" Puckerman

Most likely to get caught for inappropriate behaviour –
Jacob Ben Israel

Drama queen –
Rachel Berry

Most likely to still be at high school in six years –
Brittany

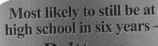

Brittany

LOOK ALIKES?

Were these McKinley High guys separated at birth from their famous twins?

Rachel Berry

Idina Menzel

Finn Hudson

Chris Klein

Sue Sylvester

Ellen Degeneres

Mr. Schuester

Justin Timberlake

Emma Pillsbury

Susan Sarandon

Noah Puckerman

The Rock

Mercedes Jones

Jennifer Hudson

Tina Cohen-Chang

Lucy Liu

ARE YOU A GEEK GEEK?

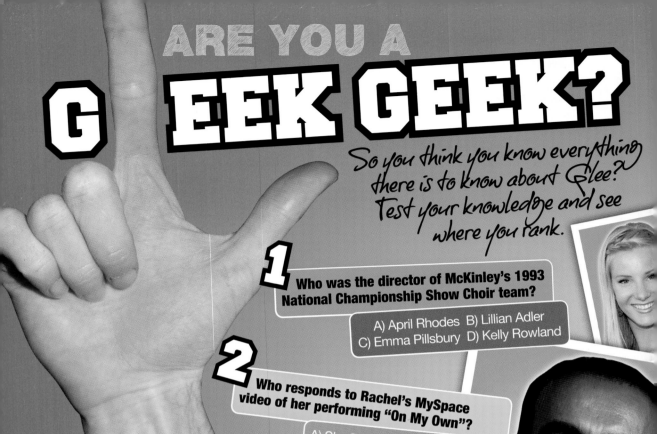

So you think you know everything there is to know about Glee? Test your knowledge and see where you rank.

1 Who was the director of McKinley's 1993 National Championship Show Choir team?

A) April Rhodes B) Lillian Adler
C) Emma Pillsbury D) Kelly Rowland

2 Who responds to Rachel's MySpace video of her performing "On My Own"?

A) Sky Splits B) Hi Ho Cheerio!
C) The Cheerios D) All

3 Which of the following brochure titles can be found in Emma Pillsbury's office?

A) Ouch! That Stings! B) Radon: The Silent Killer
C) Wow! There's a Hair Down There D) All

4 Who does Dakota Stanley call "Frankenteen"?

A) Finn B) Kurt
C) Puck D) Arty

5 What is the airline that Principal Figgins did a sock commercial for?

A) Air India B) Mumbai Air
C) Virgin Airlines D) Bombay Air

6 True or False: Jane Lynch and Kristin Chenoweth have worked together before Glee?

7 In the Director's cut of the Glee pilot, who gets an extra song?

A) Rachel Berry B) Finn Hudson
C) Will Schuester D) Quinn Fabray

8 True or False: Sue Sylvester is an American citizen?

9 What does Sue nickname Artie?
A) Wheels B) Four Eyes
C) Nerd D) Handicap

10 True or False: Matt Salling (Puck) plays guitar?

11 What difficult note is featured in "Defying Gravity"?
A) B-sharp B) High F
C) High C D) A minor

12 True or False: Jessalyn Gilsig (Terri Schuester) sings a song?

13 What does Brittany think a ballad is?
A) A vote B) A love song
C) A bullet D) A duck

14 In what other project does Stephen Tobolowsky play a character named Ryserson?
A) *Garfield* B) *Wild Hogs*
C) *Groundhog Day* D) *Sneakers*

15 What is the most popular flavour of slushie to throw at McKinley?
A) Grape B) Cherry
C) Cola D) Orange

16 What's the next competition after Sectionals?
A) States B) Regionals
C) Nationals D) World's

17 How old is Rachel Berry at the start of *Glee*?
A) 15 B) 17
C) 16 D) 18

18 Who is Finn's favourite '80s band?
A) White Snake B) Van Halen
C) Bon Jovi D) Journey

19 True or False: The show takes place in Columbus, Ohio?

20 What other show did *Glee*'s Ryan Murphy create?
A) *Nip/Tuck* B) *The Shield*
C) *Lie to Me* D) *Dawson's Creek*

ANSWERS

1) B – Lillian Adler. 2) D – All. 3) D – All. 4) A – Finn. 5) B – Mumbai Air. 6) True. 7) C – Will Schuester. 8) False. 9) A – Wheels. 10) True. 11) B – High F. 12) False. 13) D – Duck. 14) C – *Groundhog Day*. 15) A – Grape. 16) B – Regionals. 17) C – 16. 18) D – Journey. 19) False. 20) A – *Nip/Tuck*.